LIFE WORKS!

WORK IT OUT

HOW TO RESOLVE CONFLICT

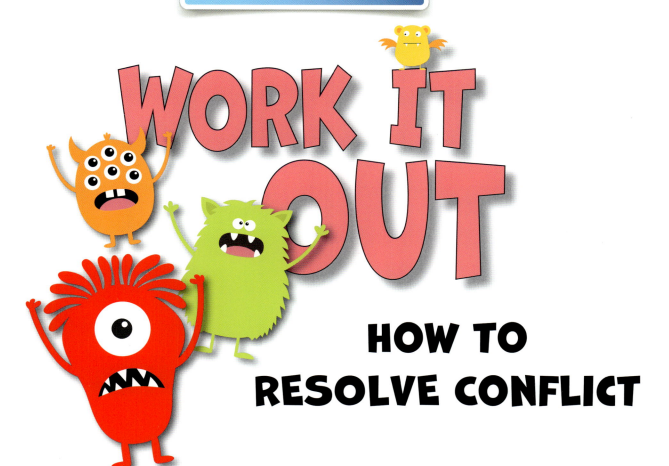

by Sloane Hughes

Minneapolis, Minnesota

Credits: 4, © zhanna tolcheva/iStock; 5, © KittyVector/Shutterstock; 6, © PCH.Vector/Shutterstock; 7, © KAMPUS/Shutterstock; 9, © Juanmonino/iStock; 15, © maryartist/Shutterstock; 16, © world of vector/Shutterstock; 16L, © FluxFactory/iStock; 16R, © FatCamera/iStock; 17, © kali9/iStock; 21, © mielag/iStock; and 22–23, © Deagreez/iStock.

Library of Congress Cataloging-in-Publication Data is available at www.loc.gov or upon request from the publisher.

ISBN: 978-1-63691-947-8 (hardcover)
ISBN: 978-1-63691-953-9 (paperback)
ISBN: 978-1-63691-959-1 (ebook)

Copyright © 2023 Bearport Publishing Company. All rights reserved. No part of this publication may be reproduced in whole or in part, stored in any retrieval system, or transmitted in any form or by any means, electronic, mechanical, photocopying, recording, or otherwise, without written permission from the publisher.

For more information, write to Bearport Publishing, 5357 Penn Avenue South, Minneapolis, MN 55419. Printed in the United States of America.

CONTENTS

Coming Into Conflict 4
Big Feelings 6
Keeping Cool 8
Take Five 10
Our Point of View 12
In The Moment 14
Understanding the Problem 16
Good Listeners 18
Give to Get 20
The Power of We 22
Glossary 24
Index 24

COMING INTO CONFLICT

We all want to get along. But sometimes the things we want and need are different than what others want and need.

When we don't agree with others, we can get into a **conflict**. This argument or fight can be **stressful**. But we can learn to work it out!

BIG FEELINGS

When conflicts happen, we often have big feelings. We can be angry or upset. That's okay!

We just have to stop and notice what we're feeling. After we name the feelings, it is easier to know what to do next.

The last time you were in a conflict, what feelings did you have?

KEEPING COOL

If we want to **resolve** a conflict, we can't let our feelings control our actions. When we do, things can get a lot worse. A conflict could turn into a big fight.

But how do we stay calm and in control? Sometimes, we need to take a break. Stop thinking about the conflict for a moment.

Taking a walk can be a good way to cool down.

OUR POINT OF VIEW

After we're calm, we can come back to the conflict. Then what? "I" **statements** help us **communicate** our point of view. They help us tell the other person what we think and feel.

I'm grossed out when I see others eating bugs.

The other person may not know something has upset us. They also may not know the reason why we've done something.

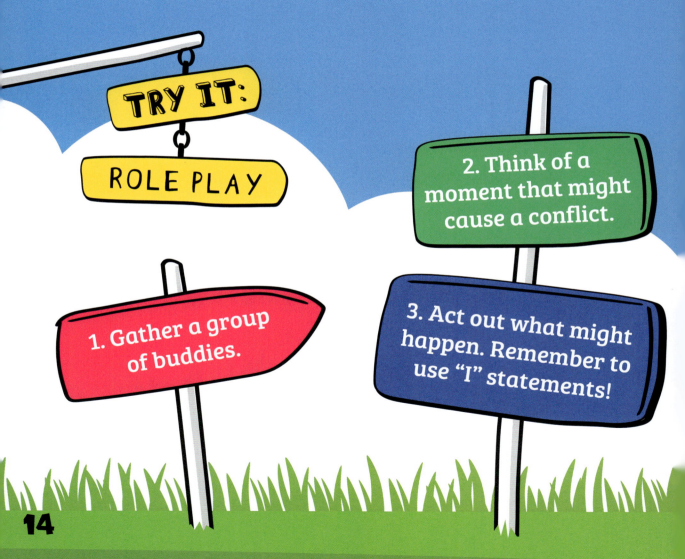

UNDERSTANDING THE PROBLEM

After we've said what we're thinking and feeling, it's time to listen to the other person's side of the story. It's important to really listen and pay attention. How do we do that?

We can put away other things.

Eye contact shows that we're listening.

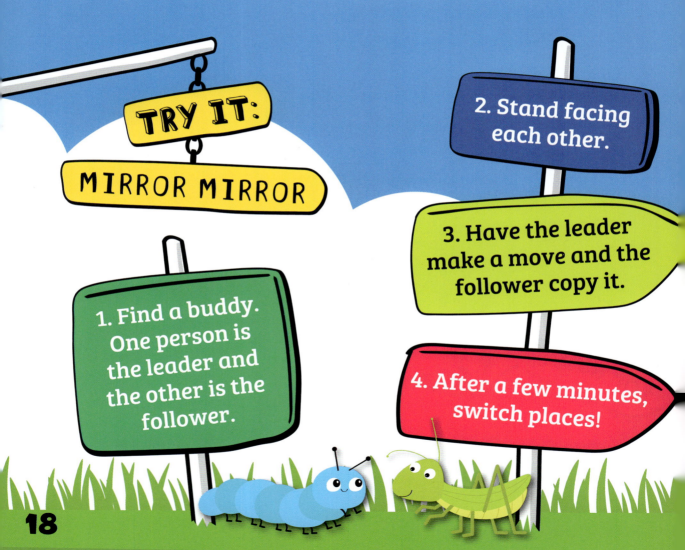

GIVE TO GET

Resolving a conflict often means finding a **compromise**. Each person gives up some of what they want.

We each give up a little, but no one loses. If we both want to play with the same toy, we might take turns. Or we could play with it together!

What is one way that giving something up can make everyone happier?

THE POWER OF WE

Together, we can find ways to resolve conflicts. When we keep our cool, conflicts aren't so bad.

We can listen!

GLOSSARY

communicate to share information, ideas, feelings, and thoughts

compromise an agreement where each side changes or gives up something

conflict a struggle where two sides do not agree

resolve to find an answer

statements things that are written or said

stressful making you feel worried

INDEX

breaks 9–10
communicate 12
compromise 20
feelings 6–8, 16
fight 5
give 20–21
I statements 12, 14
listening 16–18, 22
needs 4
wants 4, 20–21